Bear Grylls

SURVIVAL SKILLS HANDBOOK

FIRECRAFT AND CAMPFIRE COOKING

Bear Grylls

This survival skills handbook has been specially put together to help young explorers like you to stay safe in the wild. When you're spending a night in the wild, a nutritious, hot meal is a real treat, especially after a long day – but cooking outdoors can be a bit of a challenge! This book will teach you how to start a fire and rustle up some tasty treats on a campfire or camping stove. Remember: a good cook in the wild is always a popular teammate!

Bear

CONTENTS

CAMPFIRES AND COOKING

Making fire is an ancient skill that humans have practised over hundreds of thousands of years. Its discovery first set our ancestors on the path to civilization. The ability to make fire is still a vital survival skill, especially for explorers.

Invention of fire
Tens of thousands of years ago, early humans learned to make fire by striking flints or rubbing sticks together. Nowadays, we mostly use matches or lighters, but it's still handy to learn the traditional techniques, too (see pages 10–13).

Why do we need fire?
Fire is incredibly helpful. Here are just some of its many uses:

- Produces light, which is especially useful at night.
- Produces heat to warm our bodies and dry wet clothes.
- For preparing food and hot drinks.
- For purifying water.
- Provides protection against dangerous animals and biting insects.
- Provides a place to gather with friends, which boosts group morale.
- For signalling for help in an emergency.
- It is nature's TV – everyone likes to watch it!

Campfire cooking

Nothing beats the taste of a meal prepared outdoors on a campfire, camping stove, or barbecue! A hot meal is delicious after a long day's hike, and cooking your own food outdoors can be a lot of fun! Turn to pages 20–45 to find some recipes for nourishing and tasty campfire meals.

Safety warning

Fire-making and campfire cooking are great fun, but can also be dangerous. Take a lot of care around fires, and never leave a fire unattended. Always have a bucket of water or fire blanket handy so you can put out a fire if necessary. Hot cooking pots can burn you, so always use oven gloves or tongs. Beware of hot steam, which can be just as dangerous as boiling water.

BEAR SAYS

Some campsites forbid lighting fires, but you may be allowed to have a barbecue or use a camping stove. Always obey the campsite rules and be aware of the dangers of forest fires.

look out for signs telling you if fires are allowed or not

PREPARING YOUR FIRE

The key to a good fire is thorough preparation. Gather all the materials you need and stack them within reach before you begin – this will save you a lot of time and energy once you start.

Fire pyramid

A successful fire depends on three things: heat, fuel, and oxygen. Just like us humans. Remove any one of these, and the fire will go out. Vary the three factors to control your fire. For example, fan a fire to increase oxygen and make it bigger, or smother it to starve it of oxygen and make it smaller or put it out. Adding more fuel will also make your fire bigger and last longer.

Gathering materials

Assemble all the materials you need: tinder will take the spark and kindling will feed the flames. You will then need wood of different thicknesses to fuel the fire.

- **Tinder** Dry grass, straw, birch bark, sawdust, pine needles, animal fur, tissue paper, and scrunched-up newspaper all make good tinder when bone dry.
- **Kindling** Dry twigs about 2 cm across make good kindling. You can also use wood shavings, or split dry softwood with an axe.
- **Fuel** Feed the fire with small logs or split wood, then larger logs.

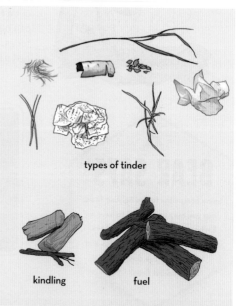

types of tinder

kindling   fuel

Choose your location

Build your fire on level ground, away from trees or overhanging branches. Site it well away from tents, and downwind of your campsite, otherwise you risk drifting sparks igniting the fabric. Clear the ground of sticks and moss that could cause the fire to spread.

BEAR SAYS

Don't use wet or damp wood on a campfire - it's hard to light and will make the fire smoky. You can dry damp tinder in your pockets and store it in a plastic bag.

Building a fire reflector

A fire reflector acts as a windshield and directs the heat for warmth and cooking.

1. Build your fire reflector upwind of your fire.
2. Hammer two stout stakes into the ground about 30 cm apart.
3. Hammer another pair about 1 m away, parallel to the first two.
4. Place long sticks between the upright stakes to form a screen.

FIRE STRUCTURES

You can build a campfire using several different structures, depending on conditions and how you want to use the fire. For example, a slow-burning, steady fire provides background warmth, while a hot fire is best for cooking.

Tepee

This simple, cone-shaped fire is quite easy to build and light. You can make a tepee fire by leaning several small sticks together above a ball of kindling to make a pyramid, or tepee, shape. This is the most basic shape for fire-lighting, and the fire can be fed with bigger logs as it burns.

Pyramid

A pyramid or temple fire uses a lot of wood but will burn for hours. Lay two large logs at the base around a small tepee fire. Place four slightly smaller logs on top, then smaller logs on top of that to form a pyramid. Light it from the side. As the fire burns down, the topmost logs will fall in to fuel the blaze.

BEAR SAYS

Place damp kindling and fuel by the campfire to dry it out, but be careful not to set it alight!

Fire pit with stones

A fire pit is very handy. It will protect a fire in windy conditions, and stop it from spreading and damaging the surrounding area. Dig a shallow pit and build a tepee fire in it. Surround the fire with a ring of stones to contain it and reflect heat.

Star shape (Seminole)

Build a tepee fire and position four large logs in a cross with their ends in the fire. Push them further in as they burn down. This structure is good if you only have large logs for fuel.

Trapper fire

Build a tepee fire between two large, green (newly cut and sap-filled) logs. These will contain the fire, preventing it from spreading, and protecting the flames from wind.

Fire platform

Lay a platform of small, green sticks underneath your campfire to protect the fire from wet ground or snow.

FIRELIGHTING

Now you've built your fire, your next task is to light it! The easiest way to do this is by using a lighter or matches, but if you don't have either to hand there are plenty of other techniques you can try.

How to light a campfire

1. Build a small tepee fire with a ball of tinder in the centre. Leave gaps so that air can reach the tinder. Strike a match or put a lighter to the tinder.
2. Blow gently to fan the ember. After the tinder has caught fire, add small and then larger sticks to feed the flames.

Using matches

Strike a match, always in the direction away from your body. Cup your hands around the flame to shield it from wind. Tilt the match head down so that it burns a little before you put it to the tinder.

Firesteel

This is a steel rod attached to a thin strip of metal called a "striker". Place the tip of the rod in the tinder and brace the striker against it. Then push the scraper down to direct hot sparks onto the tinder.

Magnifying glass

A magnifying glass will ignite dry tinder in strong sunlight. Hold the glass at an angle to direct a beam of light onto the tinder. Be patient, and eventually it will start to smoke. Blow very gently to ignite a flame.

BEAR SAYS

Firelighting can be very dangerous if you aren't careful. Never start a fire without a responsible adult nearby.

Firelighters

Firelighters are small, solid fuel packets, often soaked in flammable liquid, that you can buy in many shops. They're very useful if other techniques fail, or in windy conditions. Break the block into small pieces and place a few bits in the tinder. Wash your hands after handling firelighters.

How to make a fuzz stick

This is a partially shaved piece of wood that can be used to start a fire if tinder is in short supply. You will need a dry stick thicker than your finger. Run your penknife down the wood to create long shavings. Stop before you reach the end so that you don't detach the shavings. Always cut away from your body. Repeat this until you have several rings of shavings running up the stick.

ADVANCED FIRECRAFT

To be a true survival expert, you need to learn how to light a fire without matches or a lighter. There are several different methods. All require friction, or rubbing, to ignite the tinder. It takes a lot of patience, but it's a great skill to master!

Fire plough
You need: hardwood stick, softwood baseboard, penknife or chisel

1. Cut a long, straight groove in the baseboard using a penknife or chisel.
2. Point one end of the hardwood stick.
3. Pressing hard, repeatedly push the stick up and down in the groove. The friction will produce heat, and eventually a small ember. This ember can be added to your dry tinder, which, when gently fanned, will ignite.

Hand drill
You need: straight stick, baseboard, penknife

1. Smooth the sides of a long, straight stick, and round one end. Hold the rounded end on the baseboard near the side and draw around it. Carve a shallow, stick-sized hollow in the baseboard, then a notch at the edge. Place an ember pan or leaf under the notch to catch an ember.
2. Hold the board steady with your foot or knee, as shown. Place the stick in the hollow and roll it quickly between your palms, running your hands down the stick as you roll. Hot ember dust will fall into the notch which can be collected, tipped into your tinder, and fanned into a flame.

Flames from an ember

Once you have an ember, add it to your dry tinder, such as straw or scrunched-up paper, and fan or wave it gently back and forward through the air, until it ignites. Be gentle and don't blow too hard, or you will blow it out!

Overnight fire

To keep a campfire alight overnight, place large logs on it and cover it lightly with earth or ashes. Don't use dry leaf mould, which will make the fire flare up again.

Extinguish a fire

Allow the fire to burn right down, then sprinkle water over the embers or smother them with earth to make sure the fire is fully out.

✗

BEAR SAYS

Make sure a fire is completely out before leaving the campsite. When the ash is cold, remove any debris and sweep earth over the site.

CAMPFIRE KITCHEN

To cook outdoors, you will need pots and pans and some basic kitchen equipment. On sites where you're not allowed to have a campfire, you can usually use a barbecue or portable stove.

Stoves

Stoves are easy to light, and provide instant heat that you can control. Different designs burn gas, petrol, or solid fuel. Most are light to carry or come in a handy case. Always test the stove before your trip to make sure it is in working order, and be sure to bring enough fuel!

windshield stove

push-button stove

BEAR SAYS

Never light a stove inside a tent. This is a major fire hazard! Position your stove away from tents as you would a campfire.

Barbecues

Barbecues use charcoal, which burns hotter than wood. This makes them a good option for food that needs cooking well, such as meat. There are many designs. You can buy a disposable barbecue or even build your own using bricks and a grill.

double burner barbecue

portable barbecues

Cooking kit

A light "nest" of pans can be used on a stove, while heavy-duty pots or pans are needed to cook on an open fire. Don't bring your family's best cooking pans, as fire will blacken the outsides.

camping kettle

portable stove and light pans

portable crockery set

cooking over a campfire using a heavy pan

camping utensil sets

portable washing-up set

Cool boxes

A cool box keeps food, such as dairy products, fresh. Freezer blocks work like ice and can be refrozen on some campsites. If you don't have a cool box, you can wrap a damp towel around items such as milk to keep them cold. You can also cool bottles in a stream, but be careful they don't get washed away!

CAMPFIRE STORES

Your campfire larder should contain some basic items, plus any specific ingredients you need for each meal. Plan detailed menus in advance so that you have everything you need. Don't wait until you've started cooking to discover you've left a vital ingredient behind!

Basic stores

These basic foods will be needed for many dishes.

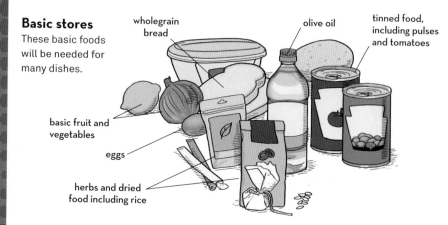

wholegrain bread

olive oil

tinned food, including pulses and tomatoes

basic fruit and vegetables

eggs

herbs and dried food including rice

Seasoning

Ingredients such as salt, pepper, and dried herbs provide flavour. You can also use stock cubes, curry spices, mustard, chilli, ketchup, or chutney to season your food.

Dried and tinned foods

Dried foods are light to carry. Canned foods are heavy but keep for a long time. Tinned pulses such as lentils, beans, and chickpeas are precooked, so are easy to use.

Wild foods

Foods found in the wild can be added to your larder. Wild garlic, oregano, mint, and basil all add flavour to food. Wild rocket is great in salads. Fruit and berries, such as apples, plums, and raspberries, can be gathered in season, as can edible fungi, like field mushrooms. Nuts, such as sweet chestnuts, can be cooked on the campfire. Be careful – you need to be absolutely sure you have identified plants, fruits, and fungi correctly, as some are highly poisonous. Do not eat anything you have found in the wild unless an adult with knowledge of plant identification says it's safe. If in doubt, especially with mushrooms, leave them out!

Balanced diet

A healthy diet should contain a wide variety of foods, including protein and carbohydrates. Fresh fruit and vegetables provide vitamins, minerals, and also fibre, which is good for digestion. A balanced diet also contains some fat and sugar, and a little salt. This pyramid shows the portions of each food you should be eating each day.

limited fat and sugar

1-2 servings dairy

1-2 servings meat, eggs, and fish

4-5 servings vegetables

4-5 servings fruit

5-8 servings whole grains

COOKING METHODS

There are as many methods of cooking outdoors – using a campfire, barbecue, or stove – as there are indoors in a kitchen. Food can be grilled, roasted, fried, boiled, or baked – plus there are some new and exciting outdoor techniques you can try.

Building a tripod

A tripod provides a sturdy support for a kettle or cooking pot. You will need three long, straight sticks. Bind one end of the sticks together with cord, and fan out the other ends and adjust to form a stable, three-legged structure. Hang a hook from the cord, then hang a pot or kettle from the hook.

Making a potholder

First, cut several notches in both ends of a long, straight stick. Then push a short, forked stick into the ground. Rest the long stick in the fork and anchor the other end to the ground firmly, using string and a tent peg. Use more string to hang a pot over your fire using the notches on the raised end.

Using a barbecue

Light a barbecue 40–50 minutes before you plan to use it. This allows the flames to die down and create a bed of glowing, red-hot charcoal on which to cook.

Spit roasting

Meat, fish, and other foods can be roasted on a spit suspended over a campfire. Use green wood to make the spit, as it is less flammable and won't catch fire. Turn the spit regularly to make sure the food is cooked thoroughly and evenly.

Baking in foil

Fish, meat, potatoes, and fruit all taste great baked in foil in the embers of a campfire. Thick foil is best as it won't tear. Wrap the foil around your food to form an airtight package. Use tongs to place it in and remove it from the fire to protect your hands. Cooking time depends on the food and size of the package. Carefully open one end of the package to check if the food is cooked. Beware of hot steam and fat escaping.

BEAR SAYS

Whatever method you use, make sure the food is cooked all the way through – you don't want to get food poisoning in the wild!

TIME FOR BREAKFAST

Exploring the wild can be hard work, so it's important to start your day with a healthy, nourishing breakfast to give you lots of energy for the day ahead.

Porridge

porridge oats
(½ cup per person)

milk or milk substitute
(½ cup per person)

cinnamon

maple syrup
or honey

banana
(sliced)

Method

1. Put the oats in a pan. Add the milk slowly, stirring with a wooden spoon. Sprinkle on the cinnamon. Bring to the boil on a medium heat.
2. Continue to cook on a low heat for about five minutes until all the liquid is absorbed, and the mixture is thick and creamy. Add a little water if the porridge is too thick.
3. Serve in a bowl with the sliced banana. Drizzle with maple syrup or honey.

1

2

3

Scottish porridge

This traditional Scottish breakfast is salty, not sweet. This version uses water instead of milk. Cook in the same way, but sprinkle a little salt on top instead of syrup or sugar.

Muesli, fruit, and yoghurt

muesli

yoghurt

your favourite
fruit

honey

BEAR SAYS

You can buy ready-made muesli
in most supermarkets, or you
could try making your own using
wheat or oat flakes, dried fruit,
nuts, and seeds.

Method

1. You can use any fruit you like for
   this, but berries, melon, grapes, and
   banana work especially well. Chop
   the fruit and place it in a bowl.
2. Add muesli and a big dollop of Greek
   yoghurt and some honey.

START WITH AN EGG

Eggs are packed with protein, which gives you energy. This makes them a great breakfast food to start the day with when you are out camping.

Scrambled eggs

3 eggs

cooking oil

seasoning

small handful peppers or mushrooms

Method
1. Break the eggs into a bowl. Add a pinch of seasoning and then beat the mixture with a fork.
2. Heat a tablespoon of oil in a pan and place on a medium heat. Add the peppers or mushrooms and cook through. Stir in the eggs with a wooden spoon to prevent the mixture sticking as it cooks.
3. Serve hot.

1

2

3

Options:
Scrambled eggs go well with smoked salmon on some wholemeal toast for a real treat.

Egg bread (French toast)

one egg
per person

cooking oil

BEAR SAYS

Remove eggs from the heat just before all the egg is set, as the mixture will carry on cooking in the hot pan.

seasoning

sliced bread

Method

1. Break the egg into a shallow dish and add seasoning. Whisk with a fork until smooth.
2. Dip one side of the bread in the mix until thoroughly coated. Flip over and coat the other side.
3. Fry a little oil in a frying pan on a medium heat. When the oil starts to sizzle, place the bread in the pan. Cook for about two minutes until golden. Flip the bread over and cook the other side. Serve hot.

1

2

3

SPEEDY LUNCHES

These tasty dishes can be whipped up on a stove or campfire for a lunchtime treat that will keep you going for the rest of the day.

Spanish omelette

cooked potatoes

cooking oil

4 eggs

½ onion

tomato

red or green pepper

tin of sweetcorn (optional)

Method
1. Slice the pre-boiled potatoes. Finely chop the onions, pepper, and tomatoes. Melt a little cooking oil in a frying pan on a medium heat. Fry the onions until golden, stirring with a spoon.
2. Meanwhile, break the eggs into a bowl, add a little milk and seasoning, and whisk with a fork. Add the chopped pepper and tomatoes.
3. Pour the egg mixture into the pan. Use a wooden spoon to make pockets in the cooked egg to allow the remaining runny egg to cook.
4. Slide a spatula underneath and flip the omelette over to cook the other side. When cooked, slide onto a plate. Cut into wedges and serve hot or cold.

1

2

3

4

Toasted bruschetta

olive oil

seasoning

wholegrain bread

tomatoes

olives

red onion

1

2

Method
1. Chop the tomatoes, onion, and olives into cubes and mix them together in a bowl. Drizzle them with olive oil and add salt and pepper if you like.
2. Toast the bread over a fire or barbecue, turning after two minutes, until both sides are browned.
3. Top each slice of toast with a big dollop of the tomato mixture. Eat straight away.

3

CHICKEN CASSEROLE AND MASH

• •

This hearty main meal is quick to assemble, but needs to be cooked slowly on a stove or campfire. Serve with mashed potatoes.

Chicken casserole

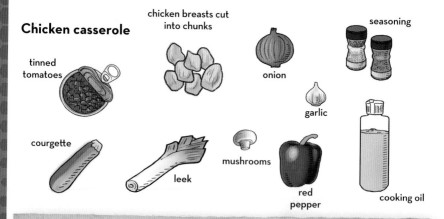

chicken breasts cut into chunks

seasoning

tinned tomatoes

onion

garlic

courgette

leek

mushrooms

red pepper

cooking oil

Method
Cooking time: About 1 hour

1. Chop the onions and vegetables and finely chop the garlic. Heat two tablespoons of oil in a large saucepan. Fry the onions, garlic, and seasoning on a medium heat.
2. When the onions start to brown, add the chicken and cook for five minutes, stirring with a spoon to make sure the meat is cooked through.
3. Now add the chopped vegetables and tinned tomatoes and mix well. When the mixture comes to the boil, turn it down. Put the lid on and cook on a low heat for about 60 minutes, stirring occasionally. Add a little water if the casserole gets too dry.

1

2

3

Mashed potatoes

potatoes

knob of butter

milk

Method

1. Peel the potatoes and add to a saucepan of cold water.
2. Bring to the boil and cook on a medium heat for about 20 minutes until the potatoes are cooked through. Remove from the heat and drain the water.
3. Add a knob of butter, dash of milk, and seasoning, and mash with a potato masher or a fork.

1

2

3

BEAR SAYS

Potatoes are very easy to cook on a campfire or stove, but are very heavy to carry, so might not be the best food if you are planning to carry it a long way.

VEGGIE STEW

This tasty and nutritious meal can be made with almost any vegetables, including ones you've foraged from the wild. As well as being warming, it's a great source of vitamins and nutrients to keep you healthy and happy on your adventures.

You will need:

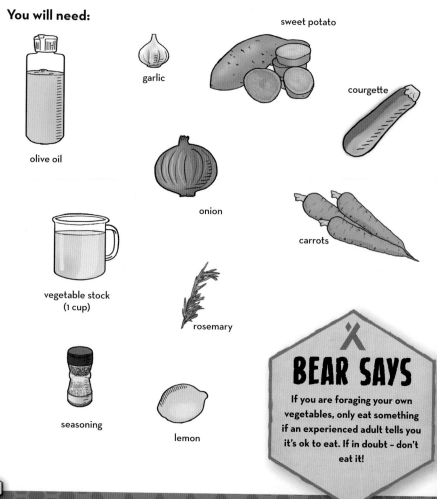

olive oil

garlic

sweet potato

courgette

onion

carrots

vegetable stock (1 cup)

rosemary

seasoning

lemon

BEAR SAYS

If you are foraging your own vegetables, only eat something if an experienced adult tells you it's ok to eat. If in doubt – don't eat it!

1

2

3

4

5

Method

1. Chop the onion and vegetables.
2. Heat a little oil in a large pan, then add the garlic and onion. Fry for around three minutes.
3. Add a cup of vegetable stock and cook for another three minutes, allowing it to simmer gently.
4. Add the chopped sweet potato, courgette, carrot, and any other vegetable you would like. Add salt and pepper to taste. Cook for 30 minutes over the campfire.
5. Squeeze in some lemon juice, give it a stir, and cook for a further 30 minutes or until the vegetables are nice and golden. Serve hot.

Tip: this recipe is delicious by itself, or with chopped chicken breast, chunks of sausage, or meat substitute. Make sure you cook any meat all the way through.

CHILLI CON CARNE

Add some spice to an evening around the campfire with this simple but tasty dish. It's traditionally cooked with minced beef, but tastes just as good with meat substitute, or just beans and vegetables. Add more chilli to make it extra fiery!

You need:

minced beef or meat substitute (300 g)

onion

garlic

fresh chilli or chilli powder

tin kidney beans

tin chopped tomatoes

wholegrain rice

cooking oil

mixed herbs

plain Greek yoghur

BEAR SAYS

Chillis can be very hot, so use with caution! You can use three tablespoons of sweet chilli sauce instead of fresh chilli or chilli powder.

Method

1. Chop the onions and vegetables, and finely chop the garlic. Heat a little oil in a pan.
2. Fry the onions and garlic on a medium heat for about 10 minutes until golden. Add the herbs, seasoning, and chilli, and cook for a few minutes.
3. Add the beef and cook for about seven minutes while stirring to brown the meat all over.
4. Add the chopped vegetables, tinned tomatoes, and meat substitute if you are using it instead of beef. Bring to the boil, then turn down and simmer on a low heat for about 45 minutes. Add the beans near the end of the cooking time.
5. Serve with rice and add a dollop of Greek yoghurt to cool it down if it's too spicy.

Quick basmati rice

1. Measure half a cup of rice per person. You will need double that amount of water. Bring the water to the boil in a pan, then add the rice. Stir once and put the lid on.
2. Cook for 10 minutes or according to the instructions on the packet. Sample with a fork to check if it is cooked, then drain away any remaining water.

BAKED POTATO MEDLEY

Baked potatoes are a campsite staple, as they're warm, filling, and easy to cook. Add a bit of variety to them by preparing a range of different fillings, and serve with a hot knob of butter.

You need:

medium-sized potatoes

butter

tinfoil

Method

1. Prick the potatoes with a fork. Smear the skins with butter and double-wrap in tinfoil. Use tongs to bury the potato in the hot ashes or coals of a campfire or barbecue.
2. Cook for 30 minutes to an hour, turning the potatoes occasionally, using tongs. Remove one potato and prod with a fork to see if cooked. When cooked, remove foil, split with a knife, and add the filling. Serve with a knob of butter and a pinch of salt and pepper.

1

2

Fillings
The great thing about baked potatoes is that they offer so much variety, with an endless list of tasty fillings you can add!

Red pepper and hummus
You need: red pepper, homemade or ready-made hummus

Chop the red pepper into cubes, removing the seeds and white pith. Top your potato with a good dollop of hummus, and sprinkle with red pepper.

Beans and salsa
You need: tin black or kidney beans, homemade or ready-made salsa

Drain the can of beans. Mix the beans into the salsa, and spoon onto your potato. This is delicious with a squeeze of lemon juice.

Goat's cheese and chive
You need: goat's cheese, chopped chives

Slice the goat's cheese and add to your potato. If the cheese is particularly soft, just add a spoonful or two. Top with a sprinkling of chopped chives.

Different flavours
Baked potatoes also taste delicious with guacamole, mushroom, and creme fraiche. This is your chance to experiment with all sorts of different flavours and ingredients. Why not try using the chilli from p.30–31? For a tasty, healthy alternative, try baking sweet potatoes instead.

BEAR SAYS

Baked potatoes take a long time to cook, so start cooking well before you want to eat. Hot ashes are very dangerous, so ask an adult to use the tongs.

GRILLED CHICKEN AND VEGETABLES

This tasty dish can be cooked in a tinfoil package in the hot embers of a campfire, or in the coals of a barbecue. You can cook almost any combination of chopped meat and vegetables in this way.

You need:

chicken breast

red pepper

courgette

broccoli

onion

chilli peppers

garlic

BEAR SAYS

Be very careful when cooking with chicken – it should be kept chilled and will not stay fresh for long.

Method

1. Cook the chicken over an open fire, or on a barbecue, making sure both sides are browned and the meat is thoroughly cooked in the middle.
2. Chop the vegetables into chunks. Then finely dice the chilli peppers and garlic.
3. Wrap the vegetables in tinfoil, adding the chopped chillis and garlic for flavour.
4. Place into the embers of your campfire carefully, using tongs. Cook for 20 minutes, then remove the foil package from the fire carefully, using tongs. Add these to your grilled chicken and eat hot, being careful of hot juices.

BEAR SAYS

If you don't fancy chicken, why not try making this recipe with fresh fish instead?

MUSHROOM AND GOAT'S CHEESE BURGERS

Burgers don't have to be unhealthy – you can cook up some delicious, healthy burgers on a campfire with just a few ingredients.

You need:

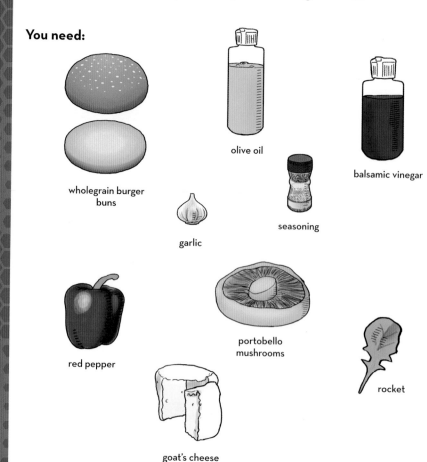

wholegrain burger
buns

olive oil

garlic

seasoning

balsamic vinegar

red pepper

portobello
mushrooms

goat's cheese

rocket

Method

1. Chop the garlic and mix in a bowl with the olive oil, balsamic vinegar, and seasoning.
2. Chop the bell pepper into quarters and cover the pepper and mushrooms with the oil and vinegar mix.
3. Heat some olive oil in a pan and cook the pepper, then mushrooms, for three or four minutes each side. Remove the skin from the pepper once cooked.
4. Fill each burger bun with a mushroom and red pepper quarter, then top with goat's cheese and a generous handful of rocket. Eat straight away.

1

2

3

4

BEAR SAYS

You can also make healthy burgers using grilled chicken breast or bean burgers.

SIDE SALADS

Salad is very good for you, packed with vitamins and minerals. These side salads will go well with any of the main meals described so far, or they can be eaten on their own as a starter.

Green salad

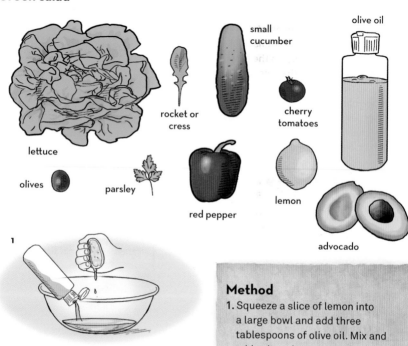

lettuce

rocket or cress

small cucumber

olive oil

cherry tomatoes

olives

parsley

red pepper

lemon

advocado

Method
1. Squeeze a slice of lemon into a large bowl and add three tablespoons of olive oil. Mix and add salt and pepper to taste.
2. Tear the lettuce and finely chop the cucumber, pepper, parsley, avocado, and tomatoes. Place in the bowl and toss until the salad is evenly coated.

Chickpea and goat's cheese salad
You need: tin chickpeas, 150 g goat's cheese, cherry tomatoes, green pepper, ½ cucumber, parsley, olive oil

Method
1. Mix three tablespoons of olive oil, a squeeze of lemon, salt, and pepper in a large bowl and mix together.
2. Drain the chickpeas. Cut the goat's cheese into cubes, chop the cucumber, pepper, and tomatoes. Add these ingredients to the bowl and toss to coat with dressing.

BEAR SAYS
You may be able to forage salad rocket, watercress, and herbs from the wild. Rocket has a peppery taste that is great in salads.

Make a vinaigrette dressing
You need: olive oil, balsamic vinegar, Dijon mustard, lemon, seasoning

Method
1. Measure six tablespoons of olive oil and two tablespoons of balsamic vinegar into a jar. Add a generous squeeze of lemon, one teaspoon of Dijon mustard, and a pinch of salt and pepper. Put the lid on and shake to mix thoroughly, or stir with a spoon.

CAMPFIRE DESSERTS

Fruity desserts taste great outdoors! These recipes provide a treat around a campfire or barbecue. A hot dessert can also boost morale if the weather turns cold or rainy.

Baked bananas

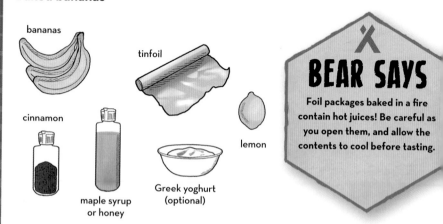

bananas

tinfoil

cinnamon

maple syrup or honey

Greek yoghurt (optional)

lemon

BEAR SAYS

Foil packages baked in a fire contain hot juices! Be careful as you open them, and allow the contents to cool before tasting.

Method

1. Peel the bananas and place in thick foil. Add a squeeze of lemon juice and a pinch of cinnamon. Close the foil to make a tight parcel. Wearing gloves, place in the embers using tongs.

2. Cook for 15–20 minutes, then remove with tongs. Carefully open the package and serve with a drizzle of maple syrup or honey, and Greek yoghurt if you like.

1

2

Fruit kebabs

honey

fruit, such as apples, pears, peaches, or apricots

long skewers

Method

1. Thread the whole, unpeeled fruit onto long skewers or peeled sticks. Wearing gloves, toast over an open fire or barbecue.
2. When the fruit skin starts to peel, remove from the heat and drizzle with honey. Return to the heat until the honey caramelizes (goes gooey). Then remove from the heat and allow to cool before eating.

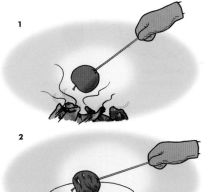

1

2

Barbecued fruit

Fruit such as plums, peaches, and apples can also be roasted on the grill of a barbecue. Cut the fruit into halves and place round-side up on the barbecue grill. Roast for three or four minutes, then turn over and sprinkle with cinnamon. Cook for another three or four minutes, then serve with maple syrup or honey and yoghurt.

MORE DESSERTS

These two simple desserts will round off an evening by the campfire perfectly – while also counting towards your five-a-day! You don't even need a fire or a stove to cook them, so they're perfect for beginners.

Campfire mess

ready-made meringues

raspberries, strawberries, or blueberries

double cream or crème fraiche

BEAR SAYS

This is a version of a pudding called Eton mess. It was invented when an excited dog squashed a dessert being delivered to Eton College, an English boarding school.

 1

2

Method

1. Chop the fruit. Break the meringues into a bowl. Whip the double cream, add to the ingredients, and stir.
2. Serve immediately.

Tutti-frutti salad

your favourite fruit – try apple, berries,
banana, grapes, pineapple, or peach

Greek yoghurt
(optional)

1

2

Method

1. Peel the fruit if necessary. Cut
   into small chunks and place in a
   bowl. Add three tablespoons of
   orange juice and mix together.
2. Serve as is, or with Greek yoghurt
   if you like.

CAMPFIRE TREATS

What better way to spend time around the campfire than swapping tales while toasting marshmallows? S'mores is a marshmallow recipe invented by Scouts on camping trips in the early 1900s.

Toasted marshmallows

marshmallows

wooden skewers
or sticks

BEAR SAYS

You can peel green, sap-filled sticks to use as skewers. Or use ready-made wooden skewers and soak them in water for at least half an hour before using.

Method
1. Thread one to three marshmallows onto sticks or wooden skewers. Toast on a campfire or barbecue for a few minutes until golden on the outside. You can prop the skewers near the fire, or wear gloves to shield your hands from the heat.

S'mores

marshmallows

thin chocolate
divided into squares

digestive
biscuits

Method

1. Toast marshmallows over a campfire or barbecue until golden. Place a hot marshmallow on a digestive biscuit. Put a piece of chocolate on top. Cover with another biscuit and squish down slightly. Serve warm. I once ate these with the President of the United States on a hiking expedition with him in Alaska! These were his favourite treat!

Fruity s'mores

Prepare in the same way as basic s'mores, but add a layer of sliced fruit sandwiched between the chocolate and the biscuit.

marshmallows

thin chocolate
divided into squares

digestive
biscuits

your choice of fruit, such as berries or banana

Extra tip

Don't hold marshmallows too close to the fire or they will burn. The gooey insides are very hot, so allow them to cool before you eat them.

GLOSSARY

• •

Brie – A soft cheese.

Caramelize – When sugar turns to a brown syrup when heated.

Carbohydrates – A group of nutrients found in foods such as fruit, vegetables, grains, beans, and dairy products. Carbohydrates provide us with most of our energy.

Ember – A glowing spark.

Firesteel – A device for lighting fires, made of a metal rod and a striker, which is scraped along the rod to produce a spark.

Forage – To look for food in the wild.

Friction – A force produced when one object rubs against another.

Fuzz stick – A stick that has been partially splintered. The splinters help the stick catch fire.

Green wood – Freshly cut, sap-filled timber that does not burn well.

Guacamole – A dip made from avocado.

Ignite – To set fire to something.

Kindling – Small fuel, such as thin sticks, used to feed a newly-lit fire.

Morale – Confidence or good spirits.

Parboil – To partly cook something, such as potato, by boiling.

Protein – A nutrient found in foods such as meat, fish, milk, eggs, nuts, and beans, that allows cells and the body to grow.

Purify – To remove dangerous substances from water.

Spatula – A cooking tool with a wide, blunt blade.

Suspend – To hang something, usually in mid-air.

Tinder – Very dry fuel used to catch a spark to light a fire.

Vegetarian – A person who doesn't eat meat.

Discover more amazing books in the Bear Grylls series:

Perfect for young adventurers, the *Survival Skills* series accompanies an exciting range of colouring and activity books. Curious kids can also learn tips and tricks for almost any extreme situation in *Survival Camp*, explore Earth in *Extreme Planet*, and discover some of history's greatest explorers in the *Epic Adventures* series.

Conceived by Weldon Owen in partnership
with Bear Grylls Ventures

Produced by Weldon Owen, an imprint of King's Road Publishing
Suite 3.08 The Plaza, 535 King's Road,
London SW10 0SZ, UK

WELDON OWEN
Editor Susie Rae
Designer Shahid Mahmood
Contributor Jen Green
Illustrator Bernard Chau
Cover image © DCL

Disclaimer

Weldon Owen and Bear Grylls take pride in doing our best to get the facts right in putting together the information in this book, but occasionally something slips past our beady eyes. Therefore we make no warranties about the accuracy or completeness of the information in the book and to the maximum extent permitted, we disclaim all liability. Wherever possible, we will endeavour to correct any errors of fact at reprint.

Kids – if you want to try any of the activities in this book, please ask your parents first! Parents – all outdoor activities carry some degree of risk and we recommend that anyone participating in these activities be aware of the risks involved and seek professional instruction and guidance. None of the health/medical information in this book is intended as a substitute for professional medical advice; always seek the advice of a qualified practitioner.

A WELDON OWEN PRODUCTION. AN IMPRINT OF KINGS ROAD PUBLISHING.
PART OF THE BONNIER PUBLISHING GROUP.